Walt Disney's MICKEY MOUSE COOKBOOK

A GOLDEN BOOK • NEW YORK
Western Publishing Company, Inc., Racine, Wisconsin 53404

Contents

8

Before You Start

Cooking can be lots of fun, especially when you're first learning how. It seems like magic—you mix up flour and milk and eggs, pour the batter into a pan, pop it in the oven, and...out comes a cake! Impossible? No, it's easy enough that you can do it in your own kitchen.

Here are the favorite recipes of Mickey and Minnie and Donald and Goofy and their Disney friends. They're all for things that you'll like to make and eat as much as they do. There are drinks and cookies for after-school snacks, cakes for parties, pancakes and main dishes that you can serve to your whole family as a special treat.

There's only one real secret you have to know to make any of the delicious dishes you'll find in this cookbook: Do *exactly* what the recipe tells you to. The reason for this is that some recipes just won't work if you change them—your cake may look like a pancake and taste like burned toast! As you become an experienced cook, you may want to experiment with a recipe, but for now you'll be happier if you follow directions.

The kitchen is a wonderful place, a place full of excitement and mystery and fun, waiting for you to discover them. But before you start to cook, there are a few simple things for you to learn. So turn the page....

Kitchen Rules

Before you start to cook, always ask if you can use the kitchen. It's nice to know that someone with experience will be around to help you or to answer your questions.

Wash your hands!

Read the whole recipe to make sure you have all the ingredients and utensils you'll need. It's no fun to start a recipe and then discover halfway through that you can't finish it because you're missing something.

When you use a knife or vegetable parer, be very careful. You should always point the blade away from yourself.

Someone older should be in the kitchen with you whenever you turn on the oven or range or any electrical appliance. Don't use them when you're alone.

Don't stand too close to the hot range or oven.

Always use potholders when you handle any hot utensil.

Turn pan handles so they don't stick out over the edge of the range. That way you won't bump into a handle and knock the pan over.

And remember to clean up when you're finished in the kitchen if you want to be welcome there again!

How to Measure

Measuring your ingredients carefully and exactly is a very important part of cooking. If you put too much or too little of something in a recipe, the food may not turn out the way you want it to, and it may not taste good. It's easy to learn how to measure ingredients, though—follow the instructions that follow, and you'll be an expert in no time.

To Measure Liquids

Fill measuring spoons right to the top, but don't let the liquid overflow. Use a measuring cup that's meant for liquids (one that's transparent and has amounts marked on the side). Put the cup on a level surface, then pour in as much liquid as the recipe calls for. Look through the cup with your eye at the same level as the liquid to make sure you have the right amount.

To Measure Dry Ingredients (Flour, Sugar, Salt, and so on)

Whether you use measuring spoons or measuring cups meant for dry ingredients, you measure the same way. Work over a piece of waxed paper. Gently fill the spoon or cup to overflowing with the ingredient. Don't pack it down or bang the spoon or cup. Then level the ingredient off with a spatula or table knife.

To Measure Margarine

Measurements for margarine are marked on the paper it is wrapped in. Put the stick of margarine on the paper and cut at the line that shows the amount you need.

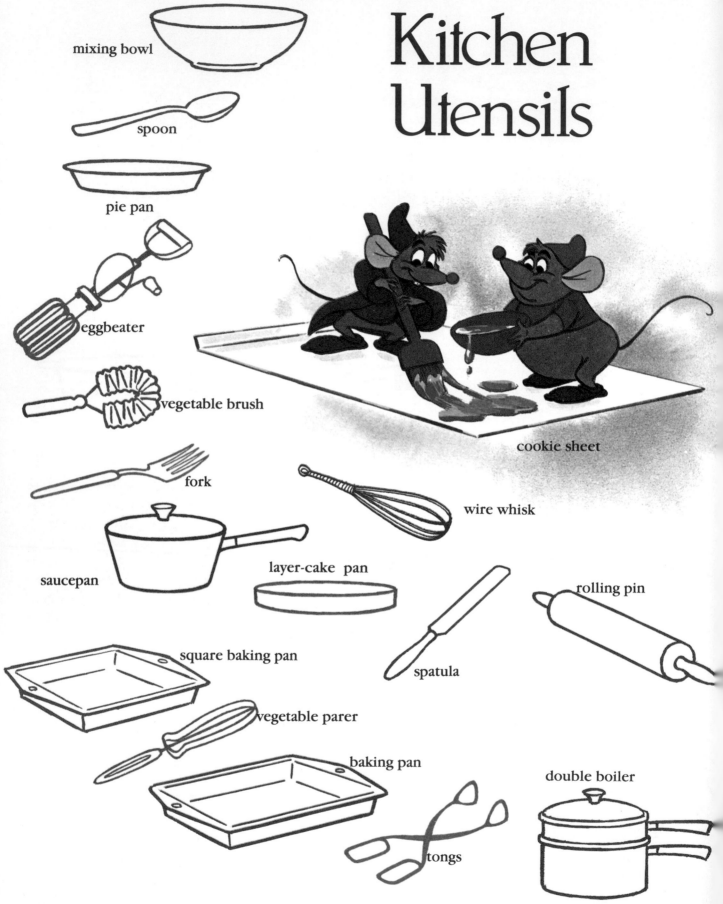

mixing bowl

Kitchen Utensils

spoon

pie pan

eggbeater

vegetable brush

cookie sheet

fork

wire whisk

saucepan

layer-cake pan

rolling pin

square baking pan

spatula

vegetable parer

baking pan

double boiler

tongs

casserole

skillet

custard cups

strainer

muffin pan

baking dish

long-handled fork

long-handled spoon

colander

loaf pan

table knife

sharp knife

pancake turner

cookie cutters

potato masher

ladle

wire rack

slotted spoon

kitchen shears

blender

15

CAKES,

CO

Frostings and OKIES

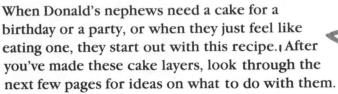

Bake-a-Cake

When Donald's nephews need a cake for a birthday or a party, or when they just feel like eating one, they start out with this recipe. After you've made these cake layers, look through the next few pages for ideas on what to do with them. Or use your imagination!

What you need:

Margarine (for greasing cake
    pans)

2½ cups sifted cake flour

4 teaspoons baking powder

½ teaspoon salt

1¼ cups sugar

2 eggs

¾ cup (12 tablespoons, or 1½
    sticks) margarine, softened

¾ cup milk

1 teaspoon vanilla extract

What you do with it:

1. Preheat oven to 350°. Grease 2 9-inch round layer-cake pans with a little bit of margarine.

2. Mix the flour, baking powder, salt, and sugar together, then sift them into a bowl.

3. Break the eggs into a large bowl. Add the margarine, milk, and vanilla and beat with a spoon until light and fluffy.

4. Stir the flour mixture into the egg mixture a little at a time, then beat with an eggbeater until the batter is creamy.

5. Pour the batter into the cake pans, making sure you get the same amount in each so that the layers will be the same thickness.

6. Place the pans on the center rack of the oven. Bake for 25 to 30 minutes. Cool in the pans 5 minutes, then circle a knife around the edges of the layers and turn them upside down onto a wire rack to finish cooling.

Makes 2 9-inch cake layers.

Once the layers are cool, you can put your cake together and decorate it. For the frosting, make one of the recipes on pages 24-25 or use canned frosting. If you wish, divide all the frosting ingredients in half and frost only the middle and the top, not the sides, of your cake.

The Mad Hatter's Un-Birthday Cake

As the Mad Hatter and March Hare knew, un-birthday parties are much better than birthday parties because you can have lots more of them. Make this cake the next time you want to celebrate your un-birthday—which comes 364 times each year (365 in leap years)!

What you need:

2 9-inch cake layers (page 18)

One of the frostings on pages 24-25 or canned frosting

Frosting-filled cake-decorating tubes

What you do with it:

1. Place 1 cake layer on a plate. Spread with some of the frosting, then put the other cake layer on top.

2. Frost the side and top of the cake with the rest of the frosting.

3. Use the decorating tubes to write "Happy Un-Birthday" on the top of the cake and to make any other designs you like.

4. Stick in as many birthday candles as you want (you can be any age on your un-birthday). Light the candles and bring the cake to the table.

19

Goofy's Fruit-Top Cake

What you need:

2 9-inch cake layers (page 18)

One of the frostings on pages 24-25 or canned frosting

1 can (8¼ ounces) pineapple slices, drained

1 small banana, cut into thin slices

6 to 8 maraschino cherries

Snow White's Sugar Glaze (page 25)

What you do with it:

1. Place 1 cake layer on a plate. Spread with some of the frosting, then put the other cake layer on top.

2. Frost the side of the cake. *Don't frost the top.*

3. Place the pineapple rings on top of the cake in a circle around the edge.

4. Pile the banana slices in the center of the cake. Top the cake with the cherries.

5. Pour the glaze on top of the fruit. Let it set for 1 hour before serving the cake.

Morty and Ferdie's Merry-Go-Round Cake

What you need:

2 9-inch cake layers (page 18)

One of the frostings on pages 24-25 or canned frosting

Colored drawing paper

6 striped plastic straws (each about 6 inches long)

24 animal crackers

What you do with it:

1. Place 1 cake layer on a plate. Spread with some of the frosting, then put the other cake layer on top.

2. Frost the side and top of the cake with the rest of the frosting.

3. Place a 10-inch dinner plate face down on the piece of colored paper. Trace around the edge with a pencil, then cut out the circle you've drawn.

4. Make 6 pencil marks equally spaced around the circle about ¾ inch away from the edge. With pencil, or a wooden pick, *very carefully* poke a hole in each of the marks.

5. Push 2 straws through 2 holes on opposite sides of the paper until about 1 inch comes out the top. With the paper attached, stick the longer sides of the straws into the cake. Put the rest of the straws through the rest of the holes and push them into the cake until 1 inch sticks out the top.

6. Stand 4 animal crackers in a circle around each straw (push them into the frosting to make them steady). When you're ready to cut the cake, remove the construction paper.

The Seven Dwarfs' Cupcakes

When seven dwarfs all have different favorite cupcake flavors, you might think it would lead to trouble. But Snow White was smart enough to think up a way to make her favorite cupcake recipe in seven different flavors. Now each dwarf gets a turn at having the kind of cupcake he wants—and so does Snow White, who thinks the plain ones are the best.

What you need:

Margarine (for greasing muffin cups)

½ stick margarine, softened

½ cup sugar

1 egg

1 cup sifted all-purpose flour

3 teaspoons baking powder

½ cup milk

1 teaspoon vanilla extract

What you do with it:

1. Preheat the oven to 350°. Grease a 12-cup muffin pan with margarine. (If you have paper muffin-cup liners, you can put one in each cup and skip greasing the pan.)

2. Put the margarine and sugar in a large mixing bowl. Cream them together until they are soft and fluffy by rubbing them against the side of the bowl with the back of a spoon.

3. Break the egg into the bowl and beat well with a fork.

4. Sift the flour with the baking powder. Add to the margarine mixture and stir. Then add the milk and vanilla. Beat with an eggbeater until the batter is smooth.

5. Pour the batter into the muffin pan, filling each cup halfway.

6. Bake for 20 to 25 minutes. Let the cupcakes cool for 5 minutes, then remove them from the pan to finish cooling (to help loosen them, circle a knife or spatula around the edge of each cupcake).

Makes 12 cupcakes.

Happy's Chocolate Chip Cupcakes: Stir ½ cup chocolate chips into the batter at the end of step 4.

Grumpy's Gingersnap Cupcakes: Crumble 8 gingersnaps and stir them into the batter at the end of step 4.

Sneezy's Raisin Cupcakes: Stir ½ cup raisins into the batter at the end of step 4.

Dopey's Nutty Cupcakes: Stir ½ cup chopped nuts into the batter at the end of step 4.

Sleepy's Cocoa Cupcakes: Beat ¼ cup cocoa powder into the batter at the end of step 4.

Bashful's Jelly Cupcakes: After filling the muffin cups in step 5, put ½ teaspoon jelly on top of the batter in each one.

Doc's Peanut Butter Cupcakes: Add 3 tablespoons peanut butter to the batter when you add the egg in step 3.

What else can you do with your cupcakes? You can frost them, using one of the recipes on pages 24–25 or canned frosting. (If the recipe makes more frosting than you need, you can divide all the ingredients in half and make less.) Then think about how to decorate the cupcakes. What designs can you make? Some things to use: frosting-filled cake-decorating tubes, raisins, candies, nuts, miniature marshmallows, coconut, colored or chocolate sprinkles, maraschino cherries.

Daisy Duck's Vanilla Cream Frosting

What you need:

½ cup (1 stick) margarine, softened

3 cups sifted confectioners' sugar

4 tablespoons milk

1 teaspoon vanilla extract

Beat in food coloring along with the vanilla to make a frosting that's any color of the rainbow. Add it a few drops at a time until you have the color you want.

Makes enough to frost and thinly fill a 9-inch layer cake (or frosts about 24 cupcakes).

What you do with it:

1. Put the softened margarine in a large mixing bowl. Cream it until it's soft and fluffy by rubbing it against the side of the bowl with the back of a spoon.

2. Slowly mix in 1 cup of the sugar. Then mix in 2 tablespoons of the milk. Mix in another cup of sugar and another tablespoon of milk. Then mix in the rest of the sugar and the rest of the milk. The mixture should be creamy so that it will be easy to spread.

3. Add the vanilla and beat with an eggbeater until the frosting is light and fluffy. If you want a softer frosting, stir in another tablespoon of milk.

Minnie Mouse's Chocolate Frosting

What you need:

4 squares (4 ounces) unsweetened chocolate

1 can (14 ounces) sweetened condensed milk

1 tablespoon water

If you like a thicker frosting on your cake, use the whole recipe (either the vanilla or chocolate) to frost the outside and use something different between the layers. Here are some suggestions: jelly or jam, fresh or drained canned fruit, peanut butter, honey.

Makes enough to frost and thinly fill a 9-inch layer cake (or frosts about 24 cupcakes).

What you do with it:

1. Fill the bottom half of a double boiler with water. Put the top half in place. Make sure that it doesn't touch the water—if it does, pour some water out. Put the double boiler over low heat.

2. Put the chocolate in the top of the double boiler and let it melt, stirring it once in a while.

3. Slowly stir the milk into the melted chocolate. Turn the heat up to medium. Cook for 4 minutes, stirring constantly, until the mixture thickens.

4. Turn off the heat. Stir in the water.

5. Let the frosting cool for a few minutes before you spread it on.

Kanga's Orange Cream-Cheese Frosting

What you need:

8 ounces cream cheese, softened

4 tablespoons margarine, softened

1 cup confectioners' sugar

½ teaspoon vanilla extract

1 tablespoon grated orange rind

What you do with it:

1. Put the cream cheese and margarine into a medium-size mixing bowl.

2. Cream them together until they are soft and fluffy by rubbing them against the side of the bowl with the back of a spoon.

3. Beat in the confectioners' sugar until everything is well mixed together. Beat in the vanilla and the orange rind.

Fills and frosts a 9-inch layer cake.

Snow White's Sugar Glaze

What you need:

½ cup confectioners' sugar

2 tablespoons milk, water, or orange juice

½ teaspoon vanilla extract

What you do with it:

1. Put all the ingredients in a small mixing bowl and blend with a spoon until creamy.

2. Pour the glaze over the top of your cake or cupcakes right away, but then let it set for 1 hour before serving.

Glazes the top of a 9-inch layer cake or 12 cupcakes.

A few drops of red food coloring mixed in with everything else make this Snow Red's Sugar Glaze. Red and blue together make it Snow Purple's. And so on.

Mickey Mouse's Sugar Cookies

What you need:

1 egg

½ cup (1 stick) margarine, melted and cooled

1 cup sugar

½ teaspoon cinnamon

2 tablespoons milk

1 teaspoon lemon juice

2 cups sifted all-purpose flour

1 teaspoon baking powder

If you only have 1 cookie sheet, bake 1 batch of cookies, then let the sheet cool before you drop and bake the rest.

What you do with it:

1. Preheat the oven to 400°.

2. Break the egg into a large mixing bowl. Add the margarine, sugar, cinnamon, milk, and lemon juice. Beat with an eggbeater until creamy.

3. Sift the flour and baking powder together into another bowl. Add this to the mixture in the first bowl and mix well with a spoon.

4. Drop the dough by the teaspoonful onto 2 cookie sheets (you don't have to grease them). Leave at least 1 inch of space between the cookies.

5. Bake for 8 to 10 minutes or until the cookies are golden brown. Immediately remove the cookies from the cookie sheets with a spatula. Place them on wire racks to cool.

Makes about 36 cookies.

The Big Bad Wolf's Brownies

What you need:

Margarine (for greasing baking pan)

½ cup (1 stick) margarine

2 squares (2 ounces) unsweetened
   chocolate

1 cup sugar

½ cup unsifted all-purpose flour

1 teaspoon baking powder

1 teaspoon vanilla extract

2 eggs, lightly beaten

½ cup pecan or walnut pieces, raisins,
   or salted peanuts

1. Preheat oven to 350°. Grease a 9x9x2-inch baking pan with margarine.

2. Melt the margarine and chocolate in a large saucepan over very low heat. Remove the saucepan from the heat.

3. Stir in the sugar, flour, baking powder, vanilla, and eggs and beat well with an eggbeater. Stir in the nuts.

4. Pour the batter into the baking pan. Bake for 30 minutes.

5. Remove the pan from the oven and place it on a rack. When the brownies are cool, cut them into squares.

Makes about 16 brownies.

How to Make Cut-Out Cookies

You can make all kinds of cookie shapes with cookie cutters. They come in many designs and work very well. Press the cutter down on the rolled-out dough. Cut out as many cookies as you can, then carefully remove the extra dough from around the cookies. Carefully remove the cookies with a wide spatula and put them on a greased cookie sheet. Roll out the extra dough again to make more cookies in the same way. In place of a cookie cutter, you can use the edge of a glass. So that the dough won't stick, always moisten the cutter or glass with water for cutting out Geppetto's Gingerbread Cookies (page 30); dip the cutter or glass in flour for cutting out Wendy's Molasses Cookies (page 31).

You don't have to rely on cookie cutters to make the shapes you like. Here's a way for you to make any shape cookie you wish: On a piece

of heavy paper, draw or trace a design or character that you'd like to see made into a cookie. Then cut it out. Place your cut-out pattern on the rolled-out dough. Using a wooden pick, pierce holes in the dough along the outline of the pattern. These holes should be close together. Then lift the pattern from the dough. Cut with a knife along the line formed by the holes. Use a wide spatula to gently lift the cut-out cookie away from the rest of the dough and put it on a greased cookie sheet.

When you've cut out all the cookies you have room for, you'll have some leftover dough. Don't waste it—shape it into a ball, roll it out again, and cut out other shapes. (If the dough becomes too dry to roll, moisten your rolling pin with a little water.)

Geppetto's Gingerbread Cookies

What you need:

Margarine (for greasing cookie sheets)

1 package (14.5 ounces) gingerbread mix

¼ cup milk

¼ cup salad oil

It's nice to have 2 cookie sheets so that you can bake the cookies all at once. If you only have 1, though, cut out and bake half the cookies. Remove them from the sheet and let it cool. Then grease it again with margarine. Cut out the rest of the cookies and bake them.

Before putting the cookies into the oven, try adding some of these tasty decorations to the tops to make faces or clothes or pretty designs: crushed peanuts, candies, raisins, miniature marshmallows, chocolate chips, coconut, sprinkles. How many more can you think of? You can also decorate the cooled baked cookies with frosting-filled cake-decorating tubes.

What you do with it:

1. Preheat the oven to 350°. Grease 2 cookie sheets with a little margarine.

2. Pour the gingerbread mix into a large mixing bowl. Add the milk and oil and mix well with a spoon.

3. Remove the dough from the bowl and shape it into a round. Wrap it in waxed paper or plastic wrap. Chill it in the refrigerator until it's firm, about 1 hour.

4. Place the dough on a lightly floured surface. Roll it out with a rolling pin until it's about ¼-inch thick.

5. Cut out cookies (see pages 28-29) and place them on the cookie sheets with a wide spatula. Leave some room between cookies.

6. Bake for 12 minutes. Let the cookies cool on the cookie sheet.

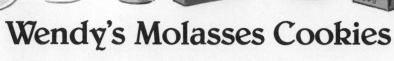

Wendy's Molasses Cookies

Everyone who lives in the secret room beneath the hollow tree in Never Land always keeps a few of these cookies tucked away in a pocket in case hunger should suddenly strike in the midst of an adventure. Not a bad idea.

What you need:

Margarine (for greasing cookie sheets)

½ **cup (1 stick) margarine or butter, softened**

½ **cup sugar**

½ **cup light or dark molasses**

1 egg

3 cups sifted all-purpose flour

¼ **teaspoon baking soda**

½ **teaspoon salt**

½ **teaspoon cinnamon**

What you do with it:

1. Preheat the oven to 375°. Grease 2 cookie sheets with a little margarine.

2. Put the margarine in a large mixing bowl. Cream it until it's soft and fluffy by rubbing it against the side of the bowl with the back of a spoon.

3. Add the sugar and molasses. Break the egg into the bowl. Mix thoroughly.

4. Sift the flour, baking soda, salt, and cinnamon together into another bowl. Add this a little at a time to the mixture in the first bowl, mixing well.

5. Remove the dough from the bowl and shape it into a round. Wrap it in waxed paper or plastic wrap. Chill it in the refrigerator until it's firm, about 2 hours.

6. Place the unwrapped dough on a lightly floured surface. Roll it out with a rolling pin until it's about ⅛-inch thick.

7. Cut out the cookies (see pages 28-29) and place them on the cookie sheets with a wide spatula. Don't place the cookies too close to one another.

8. Bake for 6 to 8 minutes. Remove the cookies from the sheets with the wide spatula and place them on wire racks to cool.

SANDWICHES

and **soups**

Donald Duck's Hamburgers

This recipe makes just the right amount for Donald and his three nephews.

What you need:

1 pound ground beef

4 tablespoons catsup or barbecue sauce

4 hamburger buns, split in half

What you do with it:

1. Shape the meat into 4 patties with your hands. Arrange them in a large skillet.

2. Cook over medium heat for about 8 minutes (less if you like your hamburgers rare). Turn the patties with a pancake turner and spread 1 tablespoon catsup on each one. Cook for about 5 minutes more.

3. Serve each hamburger on a bun.

Serves 4.

To microwave: Shape meat into 4 patties with your hands. Place patties on a microwave dish and cook on HIGH 1½ to 2 minutes. Turn the patties with a pancake turner and cook on HIGH for 2 to 2½ minutes (less if you like them rare). Serve each hamburger on a bun with a tablespoon of catsup on each one.

Scrooge McDuck's Cheeseburgers

Cash in on Uncle Scrooge's generosity and share his cheeseburger recipe—free!

What you need:

1 pound ground beef

4 hamburger buns, split in half

4 slices American cheese or mozzarella cheese

What you do with it:

1. Shape and cook the hamburger patties, following the directions in the recipe for Donald Duck's Hamburgers above, except—leave out the catsup.

2. Place each cooked patty on a bun, then top with a slice of cheese. Close the bun.

3. Wrap each cheeseburger in aluminum foil. Place in a clean skillet over medium heat and cook for 5 minutes or until the cheese melts.

Serves 4.

To microwave: Follow the instructions above. When the patties are done, top each one with a slice of cheese and let stand a minute or so until the cheese is melted. Place each patty on a bun.

Pluto's Chicken Hot Dogs

What you need:

2 chicken frankfurters

Mustard

2 frankfurter buns, split in half

Sauerkraut (if you like)

What you do with it:

1. Fill a saucepan half full with water. Place it over medium-high heat until the water boils

2. Put the frankfurters in the boiling water and cook them for 5 minutes.

3. Spread mustard on the insides of the buns.

4. Remove the frankfurters from the water with tongs. Place them in the buns. Top with some sauerkraut.

Serves 2.

Cinderella's Grilled Cheese Sandwich

When Cinderella spent so much time sitting by the cinders of the fire to keep warm, she often toasted some cheese for her supper. Here's a simple way to have melted cheese—much easier than using a fireplace!

What you need:

1 or 2 slices American cheese

2 slices bread

1 tablespoon margarine

What you do with it:

1. Place the cheese between the bread slices.

2. Melt the margarine in a small skillet over low heat. Tilt the skillet to cover the bottom with the melted margarine.

3. Place the sandwich in the skillet. Cook until the bottom slice of bread is lightly browned. Turn the sandwich with a pancake turner and cook until the other side of bread is lightly browned. When the sandwich is done, the cheese will be melted. Lift the sandwich out of the skillet with the spatula.

Serves 1.

To microwave:

1. Toast the bread and spread it lightly with margarine if you like. Put the cheese between the slices of bread with the margarine side in.

2. Put the sandwich diagonally in the center of a paper towel and fold the corners of the towel to the middle, covering the sandwich like an envelope. Place it folded side down on a microwave plate. Microwave on HIGH 30 to 45 seconds, until the cheese is melted.

You can make a Grilled Cheese and Tomato Sandwich by adding 2 slices of tomato on top of the cheese before cooking.

Piglet's Pizza Muffins

Something like this can be awfully cheering when you're feeling Very Small and rather sad about it.

What you need:

2 English muffins

½ cup Tinker Bell's Spaghetti Sauce (page 55) or bought spaghetti sauce

4 slices mozzarella cheese

What you do with it:

1. Preheat the oven to 400°.

2. Split the muffins in half by prying them apart gently around the edges. Place them split sides up in a shallow baking dish.

3. Spoon the spaghetti sauce onto the muffins, spreading it to the edges.

4. Top each muffin with a slice of cheese. (Trim the cheese slices so they're the same size as the muffins—otherwise the cheese will melt all over and make a mess.)

5. Bake for 8 to 10 minutes or until the cheese is browned slightly at the edges.

Serves 2.

Dumbo's Peanut Butter Sandwich Deluxe

What you do:

1. Spread some peanut butter on a slice of bread. Top with another slice of bread. Couldn't be easier! But—almost everybody likes a little something extra along with their peanut butter. So...

2. Before you close up your sandwich, add one of the following. Pick your usual, or see if you can find a new favorite:

Jelly
Jam
Marmalade
Apple butter
Sliced or mashed banana
Cooked bacon
Honey
Sliced apple
Grated raw carrot
Shredded coconut
Dried fruit (apricots, peaches, pears, figs, raisins, prunes, dates)
Grated Cheddar cheese
Bologna

Don't forget—toasting the bread for your sandwich is another thing you can do to make it taste different.

Chip and Dale's Triple-Decker Sandwich

What you need:

3 slices whole-wheat bread

1 tablespoon margarine

1 lettuce leaf

2 or more slices turkey, chicken, ham, or Archimedes' Meat Loaf (page 57)

2 teaspoons mayonnaise or mustard

2 slices tomato

What you do with it:

1. Toast the bread in the toaster.

2. Spread 1 side of each slice of toast with margarine.

3. Place 1 slice of toast on a plate, margarine side up. Put the lettuce leaf on top, then half of the meat slices. Spread on half of the mayonnaise.

4. Place the second slice of toast on top, margarine side up. Cover with the tomato slices and the rest of the meat. Spread with the rest of the mayonnaise.

5. Top with the last piece of toast, margarine side down. Cut the sandwich in half diagonally.

Serves 1.

Robin Hood's Meat Sandwich

What you do:

1. Choose any meat—either sliced leftover cooked chicken, turkey, roast beef, or ham; or pot roast or corned beef; or a combination of meats. You'll also need 2 slices of bread. Use your favorite kind, or try something different for a change.

2. Spread 1 slice of the bread with margarine, mustard, catsup, or mayonnaise—whatever you think will taste good with the meat you're using.

3. Place several slices of meat on the bread and top with a lettuce leaf. Cover with the second slice of bread.

Serves 1.

Some pickles or olives might taste good with your sandwich. So would some raw carrot sticks or zucchini sticks.

Pinocchio's Pea Soup With Cheese Crackers

What you need:

1 can (11½ ounces) condensed green pea soup

1 cup small cheese crackers or a couple of handfuls of cheese popcorn

What you do with it:

1. Open the can of soup and pour the contents into a saucepan.

2. Fill the empty soup can with water and add to the soup. Beat with an eggbeater until smooth.

3. Cook the soup over medium heat until hot, about 4 minutes, stirring often. To serve, pour into soup bowls and drop in the cheese crackers or popcorn.

Serves 2 to 4.

40

Baloo's Microwave Vegetable Soup

What you need:

1 can (10½ ounces) mixed vegetable juice, the spicy kind if you like it

¼ cup plus 2 tablespoons potatoes cut into ¼-inch-square pieces

1 cup frozen cut-up mixed vegetables

What you do with it:

1. Open the can of vegetable juice. Pour the juice into a 4-cup microwave container. Add the potatoes. Cover with plastic wrap and turn wrap back a little. Microwave on HIGH 5 minutes.

2. Carefully take off the plastic wrap and stir the vegetables into the soup. Cover. Microwave on HIGH 12 minutes.

3. Remove the plastic. Serve the soup in bowls or mugs.

Serves 2.

Jiminy Cricket's Yankee Noodle Dandy

What you need:

1 can (10½ ounces) condensed chicken-
noodle soup

2 cooked chicken frankfurters or 4 to 6
Lady and the Tramp Chickenballs
(page 56)

What you do with it:

1. Open the can of soup and pour the
contents into a saucepan.

2. Fill the empty soup can half full of water.
Add the water to the soup and stir.

3. Cook the soup over medium heat for 5
minutes.

4. Cut the chicken frankfurters into thin
slices and add to the soup or add the
chickenballs.

5. Turn off the heat and cover the saucepan.
Let stand for about 3 minutes before serving.

Serves 2 to 4.

Mickey Mouse's Beanie-Weenie Soup

What you need:

2 cooked frankfurters

1 can (11¼ ounces) condensed bean
with bacon soup

What you do with it:

1. Cut the frankfurters into thin slices.

2. Open the can of soup and pour the
contents into a saucepan.

3. Fill the empty soup can with water. Add
the water to the soup and stir. Add the
frankfurter slices.

4. Cook the soup over medium heat until hot,
about 4 minutes, stirring often.

Serves 2 to 4.

41

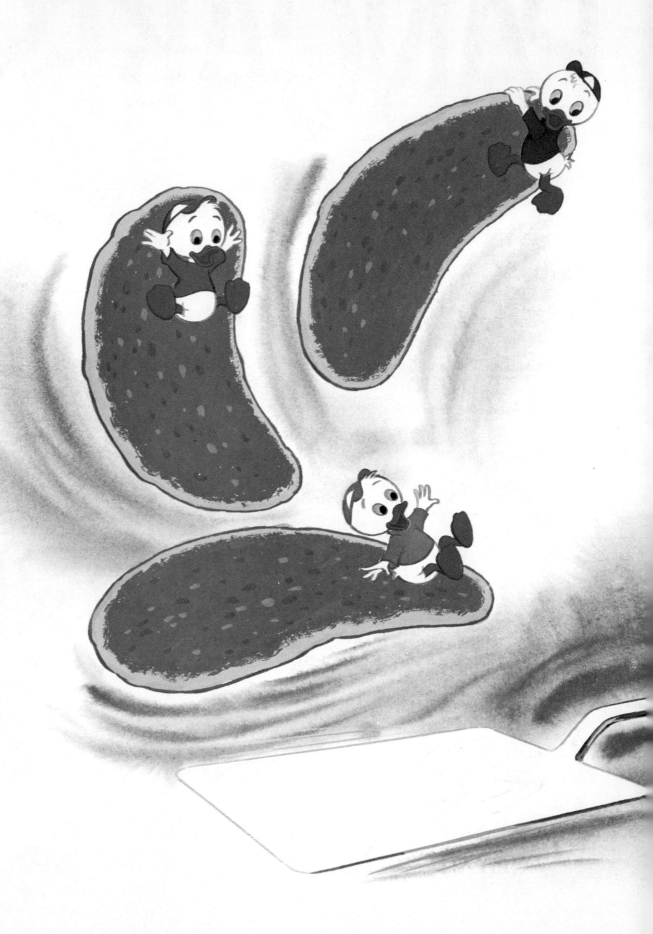

PANCAKES
and
EGGS

Wonderland Oatmeal Pancakes

There's a special trick to these unusual healthful and delicious pancakes—you make the flour yourself! Put 1½ cups regular or quick-cooking oats in the blender and blend them for about a minute, until they look like flour. You'll end up with about 1¼ cups of oat flour. Make the Orange-Honey topping the night before. Or turn the pancakes into applesauce pancakes or chocolate pancakes, or…Well, go ahead and see what kind of magic *you* can work.

What you need:

½ cup (1 stick) margarine, softened

2 tablespoons fresh orange juice

1 to 2 tablespoons grated orange rind

¼ cup honey

1¼ cups oat flour

Pinch of salt (if you like)

½ teaspoon baking powder

1 egg

1 cup non-fat milk

1 tablespoon margarine

What you do with it:

1. To make the Orange-Honey Topping: Put the ½ cup of margarine, the orange juice, orange rind, and honey in a bowl. Cream them together until they are soft and fluffy by rubbing them against the side of the bowl with the back of a spoon. Put the mixture into a small crock or serving bowl and refrigerate a few hours until it's firm.

2. To make the pancakes, combine the oat flour, salt, and baking powder in a large bowl and mix well. Put the egg and milk in another bowl and mix them well. Pour the milk mixture into the flour mixture and stir just until it's combined. Let the batter rest for 5 minutes.

3. Heat a large nonstick skillet and melt the 1 tablespoon of margarine. Tilt the skillet to cover the bottom with margarine. When the pan is hot, use a paper towel to carefully wipe out the pan. Save the towel.

4. Spoon about 3 tablespoons of batter into the skillet for each pancake. Make sure you leave room between the pancakes—be careful because the batter spreads out.

5. When the pancakes are full of bubbles but before the bubbles burst, turn them with a pancake turner. Cook until the bottoms are browned. Use the pancake turner to remove them from the skillet and stack them up on a plate. Cover the plate loosely with aluminum foil to help keep the pancakes hot.

6. Cook a second batch of pancakes the way you did the first, carefully wiping the pan with the paper towel to grease the skillet if you need it. Make a third batch the same way, and a fourth if you still have some batter left. Serve the pancakes with the Orange-Honey Topping on the side.

Makes about 8 pancakes.

The Dormouse's Applesauce Pancakes: Add ½ cup applesauce to the egg and milk after you mix them in step 2. Spread each cooked pancake with 2 tablespoons applesauce.

The White Rabbit's Chocolate Pancakes: Add 2 tablespoons chocolate syrup to the egg and milk after you mix them in step 2. When the pancakes are all cooked, stack them up in threes and drizzle 2 tablespoons chocolate syrup over each stack, or spread ½ teaspoon of apricot jam on each pancake.

The Cheshire Cat's Cheese Pancakes: Cut 1 slice American cheese into tiny strips. Add to the egg and milk after you mix them in step 2. Serve the cooked pancakes with hot pancake syrup, honey, or warm applesauce.

Tweedle Dum and Tweedle Dee's Peanut Butter Pancakes: Add 3 tablespoons of peanut butter, either smooth (Dum's favorite) or chunky (Dee's), to the egg and milk after you mix them in step 2. Sprinkle 1 tablespoon of chopped peanuts over each stack. Serve the cooked pancakes with hot pancake syrup.

The March Hare's Hot-Dog Pancakes: Cut 2 cooked chicken frankfurters into thin slices. After you pour the batter into the skillet place 4 or 5 slices on top of each pancake. Serve the cooked pancakes with hot pancake syrup.

The Queen of Hearts' Jelly Roll Pancakes: Spread your favorite flavor jelly on 1 side of each cooked pancake. Sprinkle ½ teaspoon of wheat germ on each pancake, then roll up the pancakes and fasten each one in the center with a wooden pick.

Huey's Ice-Cream Waffle Sandwich

What you do:

1. Toast 2 frozen waffles in the toaster. When done, place on a plate.

2. Cut 1 slice of brick ice cream about ½-inch thick and the same size as the waffles. Place in between the 2 waffles to make a sandwich.

Serves 1.

Louie's Fruited Waffles

What you do:

1. Toast 2 frozen waffles in the toaster. When done, place on a plate.

2. Cut up about ¾ cup of your favorite fruit and spoon the fruit over the waffles. Some good-tasting fruits are pineapple, blueberries, cherries, strawberries, apple slices, or cantaloupe. How many more can you think of? You can add crushed nuts or syrup or ice milk or ice cream to make a Fruited Waffle Sundae.

Serves 1.

Dewey's Cheese Waffles

What you do:

1. Toast 2 frozen waffles in the toaster. When done, place on a plate.

2. Spread on your favorite cheese: cottage or cream cheese, or American or Swiss cheese cut into strips.

Serves 1.

Winnie the Pooh's French Toast

What you need:

2 eggs

½ cup milk

4 slices bread

2 tablespoons margarine

What you do with it:

1. Break the eggs into a large, flat-bottomed mixing bowl or a soup plate. Add the milk and beat with an eggbeater.

2. Dip the bread in the egg mixture. Let it soak then turn it over until it absorbs all of the liquid.

3. Melt the margarine in a large skillet over medium heat. Tilt the skillet to cover the bottom with the melted margarine. Place the soaked bread in the skillet.

4. Cook until the bottom side of the bread is browned, then turn with a pancake turner and cook until the second side is browned. Remove from the skillet with the pancake turner.

Serves 2.

Tigger's Cheese French Toast: Cut 2 slices American cheese into little strips. After you turn the bread over in step 4, put the cheese on top of the bread. Cook until the cheese is melted and the bottom of the bread is browned.

Eeyore's Jam French Toast: After you turn the bread over in step 4, spread each slice evenly with jam (or jelly). Cook until the bottom of the bread is browned.

Owl's Peanut Butter French Toast: After you turn the bread over in step 4, spread each slice evenly with peanut butter. Cook until the bottom of the bread is browned.

Christopher Robin's Open-Face French Toast Sandwich: After you turn the bread over in step 4, cover each slice with a slice of chicken or ham or any favorite meat, or spread evenly with cream cheese. Cook until the bottom of the bread is browned.

If you're Pooh, you drizzle honey over your French toast before you eat it. You might like it that way, too, or you can have pancake syrup or sugar and cinnamon.

47

Sherwood Forest Scrambled Eggs

What you need:

2 eggs

2 tablespoons milk

1 tablespoon margarine

Salt and pepper

What you do with it:

1. Break the eggs into a small bowl. Add the milk and beat with a fork.

2. Melt the margarine in a small skillet over medium heat. Tilt the skillet to cover the bottom with the melted margarine. Turn the heat down to low.

3. Pour the eggs into the skillet. Cook slowly, pushing the eggs with a pancake turner as they start to set at the bottom. Cook until eggs are thickened and done.

4. Pour the eggs onto a plate and sprinkle with salt and pepper.

Serves 1.

To Microwave:

1. In a small microwave bowl melt the margarine on HIGH 30 seconds.

2. Break the eggs into another small bowl. Add the milk and beat with a fork.

3. Pour the eggs into the margarine and microwave on HIGH 1 minute. Push the eggs with a pancake turner so the firmer outside part is pushed to the middle and the less-cooked egg goes to the outside. Microwave 30 to 60 seconds more, stirring once more, until the eggs are a little bit softer than you like them. They will continue to cook after you take them out of the microwave.

Robin Hood's Scrambled Eggs With Ham: Cut 1 slice ham into small strips. Add with the milk in step 1.

Maid Marian's Scrambled Eggs With Cheese: Cut 1 slice American cheese into tiny strips. Add with the milk in step 1.

Friar Tuck's Scrambled Eggs and Mushrooms: Cut 1 or 2 mushrooms into thin slices. Add with the milk in step 1.

Little John's Scrambled Eggs With Tuna: Add 3 tablespoons broken-up tuna fish to the eggs with the milk in step 1.

49

Smee's Fried Eggs

The reason Smee is so fond of fried eggs is that every time he makes them and sees the two yellow yolks staring out at him from the skillet, he is pleasantly reminded of Captain Hook's eyes.

What you need:

2 eggs

1 tablespoon margarine

Salt and pepper (if you like)

What you do with it:

1. Break the eggs into a small bowl. Be *very* careful not to break the yolks.

2. Melt the margarine in a small skillet over medium heat. Tilt the skillet to cover the bottom with the melted margarine.

3. Turn the heat down to low and carefully slide the eggs into the skillet.

4. Cook slowly until the whites are set and a film forms over the yolks. This will take about 4 minutes. If you like the yolks cooked more, cover the pan, turn off the heat, and let stand for 2 minutes.

5. Slip a pancake turner under the eggs to loosen them. Slide them onto a plate and sprinkle with salt and pepper.

Serves 1.

50

Duchess's Baked Eggs

What you need:

Margarine (for greasing pie pan)

4 eggs

¼ teaspoon salt (if you like)

¼ teaspoon pepper

What you do with it:

1. Preheat the oven to 350°. Grease an 8- or 9-inch pie pan very heavily with margarine.

2. Break 1 egg into a cup and slide it carefully into the pie pan. Repeat with the remaining eggs, making sure the yolks don't get crowded together.

3. Sprinkle with salt and pepper.

4. Bake for 15 minutes or until the whites are set and the yolks have a film over them.

Serves 2 to 4.

Mowgli's Hard-Cooked Eggs

What you do:

1. Place as many eggs as you want to hard-cook in a saucepan, but don't crowd them. Add enough cold water to cover the eggs.

2. Cover the saucepan and cook over medium heat until the water boils.

3. Immediately turn the heat down to very low and cook for 10 minutes.

4. Remove the saucepan from the heat and let stand for 10 minutes.

5. Uncover the saucepan and place it in the sink. Let cold water run onto the eggs for a minute to cool them, then remove the eggs from the saucepan and place them in the refrigerator.

6. When the eggs are cold, remove the shells by gently cracking them all over and peeling them off carefully.

51

Peter Pan's Pasta

What's pasta? It's the name for any kind of noodle, macaroni, or spaghetti. And any kind of pasta is perfect for feeding a troop of hungry Lost Boys when they return from fighting pirates or tracking Indians—any kind, as long as there's an awful lot of it!

What you need:

1 package (8 ounces) noodles, macaroni, or spaghetti

Tinker Bell's Spaghetti Sauce (next page) or about 2 cups of your favorite bought or homemade sauce

Grated Parmesan or Romano cheese (if you like)

What you do with it:

1. Pour 3 quarts water into a pot that holds at least 6 quarts. Place the pot over high heat and let the water come to a rolling boil—this means that big bubbles quickly rise up from the bottom of the pot and break on the surface.

2. Add the pasta (remember the word?) and stir with a long-handled fork or spoon.

3. Cook, stirring occasionally, until the pasta is just tender. This will take 8 to 12 minutes, depending on the kind. The package the pasta came in will mention a time, but the only way to really know is to test: Carefully remove a piece from the pot, let it cool for a few seconds and bite into it.

4. While the pasta cooks, pour the sauce into a small saucepan and heat it over medium-low heat, stirring it once in a while.

5. When the pasta is cooked, you'll need some help from somebody older (but watch what they do so you'll know how when your time comes). Ask them to drain the pasta into a colander in the sink and shake off all the water.

6. Put the hot pasta on a serving platter and pour the hot sauce over it. Pass a bowl of the cheese at the table.

Serves 2 to 4.

54

Tinker Bell's Spaghetti Sauce

You can double this recipe and freeze what's left over until you need it for another time.

What you need:

1 tablespoon vegetable oil

¼ cup chopped onion

¼ cup chopped green pepper

2 cans (8 ounces each) tomato sauce

¼ teaspoon oregano or mixed Italian herbs (if you like)

Salt (if you like)

What you do with it:

1. Heat the oil in a medium skillet over medium heat. Add the onion and green pepper. Cook, stirring often, until the vegetables are soft.

2. Open the cans of tomato sauce and pour the contents into the skillet. Add the oregano and salt and stir.

3. Turn the heat down to low and cook for 10 minutes, stirring once in a while.

Makes about 2¼ cups.

To microwave:

1. Put oil, onion, and green pepper into a 1-quart glass measuring bowl and microwave on HIGH 3 minutes, stirring once.

2. Open the cans of tomato sauce and pour the contents into the bowl. Add the oregano and stir. Cover with waxed paper and microwave 3 to 4 minutes, stirring once in a while.

Lady and the Tramp's Spaghetti and Chickenballs

What you need:

1 egg

1 pound ground chicken or turkey (you can buy it this way)

½ cup bread crumbs or 2 slices bread, torn into tiny pieces

½ cup spaghetti sauce

1 teaspoon onion flakes

½ teaspoon salt (if you like)

Peter Pan's Pasta (pages 54-55)—use spaghetti for this recipe (and don't forget that you'll need extra spaghetti sauce and some grated cheese)

What you do with it:

1. Preheat the oven to 400°.

2. Break the egg into a large mixing bowl and beat it lightly with a fork. Add the ground chicken, bread crumbs, the ½ cup spaghetti sauce, onion flakes, and salt.

3. Mix everything together with your hands (you *did* wash them, didn't you?). Squeeze the mixture and turn it around and around in the bowl only until everything is well mixed—if you handle it too much, the chickenballs will get tough.

4. Wet your hands and shake off the extra water. Roll a heaping tablespoon of the mixture at a time between your palms to form a 1-inch meatball. Wet your hands again if they become sticky. Arrange the chickenballs next to one another (but not touching) in a baking pan, 13x9x2 inches.

5. Bake for 20 minutes. You don't have to turn the chickenballs; they will brown evenly.

6. As soon as you put the chickenballs in the oven, start cooking the spaghetti. When you add the spaghetti to the boiling water, start heating the extra spaghetti sauce. The spaghetti and the sauce should both be ready at the same time the chickenballs finish baking.

7. Put the drained hot spaghetti on a serving platter. With a slotted spoon, remove the chickenballs from the baking pan and arrange them on top of the spaghetti. Pour the hot spaghetti sauce over everything. Serve with the grated cheese.

Serves 4 to 6.

Archimedes' Meat Loaf

What you need:

1 egg

1½ pounds ground chuck or turkey

¾ cup bread crumbs or 3 slices bread, torn into tiny pieces

½ cup tomato sauce or catsup

1 teaspoon onion salt

1 teaspoon salt (if you like)

What you do with it:

1. Preheat the oven to 350°.

2. Break the egg into a large mixing bowl and beat it lightly with a fork.

3. Add the rest of the ingredients. Mix everything together with your hands (wash them first!), squeezing the mixture and turning it around and around in the bowl only until everything is well mixed.

4. Place the meat loaf mixture in a loaf pan, 9x5x3 inches. Pat the mixture evenly with your fingers to make the top smooth.

5. Bake for 1 hour. Let stand for 10 minutes. Serve from the pan, cutting the meat loaf into slices with a knife and lifting the slices out with a pancake turner.

Serves 4 to 6.

Any meat loaf that doesn't get eaten makes a delicious sandwich (something Archimedes, Wart, and Merlin know all about, since this recipe serves 6 and there are only 3 of them). Just slice the cold meat loaf and place it between 2 slices of bread—rye is very good—that you've first spread with mustard or catsup or barbeque sauce.

Donald Duck's Applesauce-Topped Ham

What you need:

2 tablespoons margarine

2 center-cut ham slices,
   ¼ to ½-inch thick

½ cup applesauce

2 tablespoons brown sugar

1 tablespoon lemon juice

What you do with it:

1. Melt the margarine in a large skillet over low heat. Add the ham slices and fry for 3 to 5 minutes on each side. (If you use precooked ham, fry for only 2 minutes on each side.)

2. While the ham is cooking, mix the applesauce, brown sugar, and lemon juice in a small saucepan and warm slightly. When the ham is ready, spread the warm applesauce on top.

Serves 4.

Merlin's Magic Fried Chicken

Merlin always has a trick or two up his sleeve. Can you figure out how he makes this fried chicken—without frying it? Give up? The oven does the "frying." Now you know a kitchen magic trick!

What you need:

1 teaspoon margarine

½ cup all-purpose flour

½ teaspoon paprika

½ teaspoon salt (if you like)

2½ pounds chicken pieces

What you do with it:

1. Preheat the oven to 425°. Grease a baking pan, 13x9x2 inches, with the margarine.

2. Put the flour, paprika, and salt in a clean plastic or paper bag that doesn't have any holes in it. Twist the top of the bag to close it. Hold it closed tightly and shake it to mix the ingredients.

3. Place 2 or 3 chicken pieces in the bag. Twist it closed again and hold it while you shake the bag to coat the chicken with the flour mixture. Count to 5 slowly while you shake.

4. Repeat, shaking 2 or 3 chicken pieces at a time until you've coated all of them. Place them side by side in the baking pan, skin sides up.

5. Bake for 40 to 50 minutes or until the chicken is golden brown on the outside and tender when you stick a fork into the thickest piece.

Serves 4.

Mickey Mouse's Microwave Macaroni and Cheese

What you need:

3 tablespoons margarine

3 tablespoons flour

½ teaspoon salt (if you like)

¼ teaspoon pepper

2½ cups milk

2 cups shredded Cheddar cheese (about ½ pound)

½ pound elbow macaroni, slightly undercooked

½ cup bread crumbs

What you do with it:

1. Put 2 tablespoons of the margarine in a round 2-quart microwave dish. Cook on HIGH 2 minutes until the margarine is melted

2. Stir the flour, salt, and pepper into the margarine. Beat in the milk with a wire whisk or an eggbeater. Microwave on HIGH 4 to 6 minutes, stirring several times, until the mixture starts to thicken.

3. Stir in 1½ cups of the cheese and stir until the cheese is melted. Stir in macaroni. Cover.

4. In a small glass bowl, mix bread crumbs and the remaining 1 tablespoon of margarine. Microwave on HIGH 1 minute, stirring once, until the crumbs are lightly toasted. Set it aside.

5. Put the macaroni in the microwave and cook on HIGH 3 minutes. Uncover the macaroni and sprinkle the remaining ½ cup cheese over the top. Sprinkle the bread crumbs over the cheese and microwave on HIGH 1½ to 2 minutes, until the cheese is melted.

Serves 3 or 4.

Thumper's Tuna-Noodle Casserole

What you need:

1 can (6½ ounces) water-packed tuna fish

1 can (8¾ ounces) green peas, or ¾ cup frozen peas

1 can (10¾ ounces) condensed cream of mushroom soup

½ cup milk

3 cups cooked noodles (6 ounces before it's cooked) (see Peter Pan's Pasta, page 54, for directions on how to cook noodles)

What you do with it:

1. Preheat the oven to 350⁰.

2. Open the tuna can. Empty the contents into a strainer held over the sink and let the water drain off. Put the tuna in a small dish. With a fork, break it up into little pieces.

3. Open the can of peas. Empty the contents into the strainer over the sink. Set the drained peas aside.

4. Open the can of soup. Empty the contents into a 1½-quart casserole and stir. Stir in the milk a little at a time.

5. Add the tuna, peas, and noodles to the casserole and stir everything together. For a different kind of tuna casserole, put pieces of Swiss cheese on top about 10 minutes before the casserole has finished baking.

6. Bake for 30 minutes.

Serves 4.

VEGET

AND

ABLES
SALADS

The Caterpillar's Corn on the Cob

What you need:

4 ears corn

What you do with it:

1. Remove the husks (outer covering) and silk (threads) from the corn. Wipe off threads by brushing up from the narrow end with a damp paper towel.

2. Place the corn in a large pot and cover with cold water.

3. Cover the pot and heat over high heat until the water begins to boil. Cook for about 3 minutes.

4. Turn off the heat. Remove the corn from the water with tongs.

Serves 4.

Serve the corn while it's piping hot, with salt, pepper, and butter.

Brer Rabbit's Carrots

What you need:

4 large carrots
2 tablespoons margarine, softened
3 tablespoons brown sugar

What you do with it:

1. Pare the carrots with a vegetable parer. Cut them into thin slices.

2. Place the carrots in a saucepan and cover with cold water.

3. Cover the saucepan and heat over medium-high heat until the water starts to boil. Turn the heat down to low, remove the cover, and cook 15 minutes longer.

4. When the carrots are tender, pour the contents of the saucepan into a colander in the sink. (Ask for help with this—*don't* do it yourself.) Shake the colander to drain off all the water.

5. Put the carrots back into the saucepan. Gently stir in the margarine and brown sugar. Cook over low heat for 2 minutes, stirring a few times. The carrots should be shiny.

Serves 4.

Grumpy's Green Beans

You'll be anything but grumpy after trying green beans the way Grumpy makes them.

What you need:

1 pound fresh green beans

1½ cups water

2 tablespoons margarine

¼ cup slivered almonds or crushed peanuts

What you do with it:

1. Wash the beans. Break or cut off the ends, then break or cut the beans into 2-inch lengths.

2. Pour the water into a medium saucepan and bring it to a boil over medium-high heat. Add the beans. (The water should cover the beans.)

3. Cover the saucepan and cook over low heat for 10 to 12 minutes or until the beans are tender but not soggy. To see if they're

done, pierce a bean with a fork or take it out of the pan and bite into it. Drain the beans in a colander or strainer (get some help with this) and put them back into the pan.

4. Add the margarine to the beans and let it melt. Stir, then empty the beans into a serving dish. Sprinkle with the almonds—they make the beans taste extra good.

Serves 4.

Captain Hook's Mashed Potatoes

The villainous Scourge of the Seven Seas uses his hook to mash potatoes, striking terror into the hearts of his crew. Since you don't have a hook, you'll just have to use a potato masher. Believe it or not, it's easier that way—and lots less messy.

What you need:

4 medium potatoes

½ teaspoon salt

½ cup milk

2 tablespoons margarine, softened

Salt and pepper

What you do with it:

1. With a vegetable parer, pare the skins from the potatoes. Rinse them off under running cold water.

2. Cut the potatoes in quarters (the pieces should all be about the same size). Put them in a saucepan and add enough cold water to cover them. Add the salt.

3. Cook the potatoes over medium-high heat until the water boils. Then lower the heat to medium and cook until the potatoes are tender when you stick a fork into them, about 30 minutes.

4. Ask someone older to drain the potatoes into a colander in the sink (watch how it's done, but don't try it yourself—you might hurt yourself). Put the drained potatoes back into the pot.

5. Mash the potatoes with a potato masher until *all* the lumps are gone, then beat in the milk and margarine a little at a time with a fork. Add a little salt and pepper and beat until the potatoes are fluffy. (Whew!) Scoop the potatoes into a serving dish.

Serves 4.

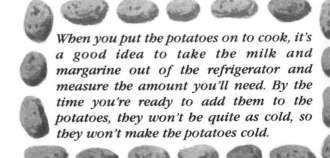

When you put the potatoes on to cook, it's a good idea to take the milk and margarine out of the refrigerator and measure the amount you'll need. By the time you're ready to add them to the potatoes, they won't be quite as cold, so they won't make the potatoes cold.

Daisy Duck's Baked Potatoes

What you do:

1. Preheat the oven to 375°.

2. Use 1 baking potato for each person you want to serve. Scrub the potatoes under running cold water with a vegetable brush to get off all the dirt. Pat them dry with paper towels. Stick each potato in a couple of places with a fork (so that they won't explode when you bake them!).

3. You can bake the potatoes right on the oven rack, or you can put them in a baking pan if you'd rather. Bake them for 1 hour, then test to see if they're done: If you can stick a fork into them easily, they're ready to eat. If they're still a little hard, put them back in the oven and try them again in 15 minutes.

4. Cut 2 slits in each potato, one going the long way, the other crossing it the short way. With a pot holder, gently press the ends of the potato toward the center until some of the insides pop up through the opening.

Top your potatoes with butter or sour cream. Or what about trying something new? Cream cheese? Cooked broccoli pieces and sliced cheese? Crumbled bacon? Tuna fish and mayonnaise? Almost anything!

Bambi's Garden Salad

What you need:

1 head bibb or Boston lettuce, separated into leaves (if head is small, use 2)

2 large tomatoes

Salt and pepper

¼ cup of your favorite salad dressing

Carrot Curls, Celery Brushes, or Cucumber Wheels (this page)

What you do with it:

1. Wash the lettuce leaves and tomatoes, then pat dry with paper towels.

2. Tear the lettuce into bite-size pieces and put it in a large salad bowl. Sprinkle with salt and pepper.

3. Cut the tomatoes into wedges and put them in the bowl. Pour the dressing over the salad.

4. Toss gently with 2 spoons until all the lettuce is coated with dressing. Top the salad with 1 or 2 of the vegetable garnishes if you want to.

Serves 4.

Carrot Curls

What you do:

Wash 1 or 2 carrots and pare with a vegetable parer. Using the parer, cut the carrot into long, thin strips. Roll each strip around your finger to make a curl, then fasten it with a wooden pick. Place in a bowl of ice water in the refrigerator for 1 hour. (Throw away the wooden picks before you add the curls to the salad!)

Celery Brushes

What you do:

Cut 2 celery stalks into 2-inch pieces. Make 4 or 5 cuts, ¾-inch long, next to one another in each end of each piece. Place in a bowl of ice water in the refrigerator for 1 hour.

Cucumber Wheels

What you do:

Wash 1 large cucumber. With the tines of a fork, carefully make lines all the way down the cucumber (the tines will cut through the peel and let the light-green part of the cucumber show through). Slice the cucumber crosswise to make wheels.

O'Malley's Tuna Fish Salad

O'Malley used to eat his tuna fish plain. Then he took up with Duchess, and ever since, his taste in food has been awfully fancy for an alley cat. This salad is one of his specialties.

What you need:

1 can (3¼ ounces) water-packed tuna fish

2 teaspoons mayonnaise

¼ teaspoon onion salt

1 stalk celery

2 lettuce leaves

What you do with it:

1. Open the can of tuna fish and drain it into a strainer held over the sink.

2. Put the drained tuna in a small mixing bowl with the mayonnaise and onion salt.

3. Cut the celery stalk into tiny pieces and put them in the bowl with the tuna.

4. Mix everything together. If you like your tuna salad creamier, you can mix in some more mayonnaise.

5. Place a lettuce leaf on each of 2 salad plates. Spoon the salad onto the center of each leaf.

Serves 2.

You can fancy up your tuna salad even more by stirring in some cut-up pickles, tomatoes, olives (either green or black), or cut-up red cabbage.

King Louie's Fruit Salad

This tastes so good that you'll be lucky if no one takes off with the ingredients before you finish making the recipe!

What you need:

1 can (8½ ounces) grapefruit sections

1 can (8¼ ounces) pineapple chunks

2 bananas

¼ cup orange juice

1 teaspoon lemon juice

4 lettuce leaves

4 maraschino cherries (if you like)
   or cottage cheese

What you do with it:

1. Open the cans of grapefruit and pineapple. Drain them into a strainer held over the sink. Put the fruit in a small mixing bowl.

2. Peel the bananas and cut into thin slices. Put them in the bowl with the fruit.

3. Pour in the orange juice and lemon juice. Stir gently. Cover the bowl with plastic wrap and put it in the refrigerator to chill for 1 hour.

4. Place 1 lettuce leaf on each of 4 salad plates. With a slotted spoon, divide the fruit among the plates. Top each salad with a cherry or some cottage cheese.

Serves 4.

Owl's Orange Pudding

What you need:

1 package (about 3½ ounces) instant vanilla pudding

2 cups milk

½ cup shredded coconut

1 cup drained canned mandarin orange sections

What you do with it:

1. Read the directions on the back of the pudding package. Follow them to make the pudding, using the milk.

2. Add the coconut and orange sections and mix.

3. Divide the pudding among 4 dessert dishes. Chill in the refrigerator until set, about 15 minutes.

Serves 4.

74

Jiminy Cricket's Cherry Vanilla Freeze

What you need:

8 maraschino cherries

1 package (about 3½ ounces) instant vanilla pudding

2 cups milk

What you do with it:

1. Cut each cherry in half.

2. Read the directions on the back of the pudding package. Follow them to make the pudding, using the milk.

3. Add the cherries and stir.

4. Divide the pudding among 4 dessert dishes. Place in the freezer for 1 hour.

Serves 4.

Winnie the Pooh's Microwave Custard

Pooh rather likes this for dessert on a very cold and blustery day.

What you need:

3 eggs

3 cups milk

½ cup sugar

½ teaspoon vanilla or lemon extract

What you do with it:

1. Break the eggs into a 5- or 6-cup glass bowl and beat lightly with a fork. Add the milk and sugar and beat again, until it is well mixed.

2. Microwave on HIGH 4 to 6 minutes, stirring every 2 minutes, just until the custard starts to thicken (it will continue to cook after you take it out of the microwave). Stir in vanilla or lemon extract.

3. Pour custard into 6 custard cups, cover the cups with waxed paper, and let the custard cool and set completely.

Serves 6.

Alice's Applesauce Fluff

If you put your ear close to a dish of this and listen very carefully, you *may* hear it whispering softly, "Eat me!" Then again, you may not—but you never know....

What you need:

½ cup boiling water

1 envelope unflavored gelatin

2 tablespoons sugar

½ cup cold water

2 cups applesauce

What you do with it:

1. Pour the boiling water into a large mixing bowl. (It's easier if you measure out ½ cup water first and boil it in a small saucepan.) Add the gelatin and sugar. Stir until they dissolve.

2. Add the cold water and stir. Add the applesauce and stir again.

3. Put the bowl in the refrigerator and chill until the mixture is thickened. It should be quivery but not firm. This will take about 45 minutes.

4. Beat with an eggbeater until the mixture is light and fluffy. Divide it among 6 dessert dishes. Put them in the refrigerator and chill until the fluff is firm, about 1 hour.

Serves 6.

It's nice to plop a spoonful of cut-up strawberries, if you have any, on each portion of the fluff. Or you can sprinkle on some cinnamon.

76

Scrooge McDuck's Blueberry Crunch

What you need:

Margarine (for greasing baking dish)

2 cups cornflakes

2 cups blueberries

½ cup sugar

¼ cup water

1 tablespoon lemon juice

2 tablespoons margarine, melted

What you do with it:

1. Preheat oven to 375°. Grease a 1½-quart baking dish with margarine.

2. Put the cornflakes between two pieces of waxed paper and crush them into little pieces with the bottom of a glass. Set them aside.

3. Wash and drain the blueberries and put them in a medium saucepan. Add the sugar, water, and lemon juice. Cover and cook for 5 minutes over low heat.

4. Pour half the blueberry mixture into the baking dish and top with half the crushed cornflakes. Pour the rest of the blueberry mixture into the baking dish, then top with the rest of the crushed cornflakes. Drizzle the melted margarine on top.

5. Bake for 25 minutes. Serve warm.

Serves 4.

Ice milk or ice cream are really good on top of the crunch—but it's good without them, too.

You can make all kinds of fruit crunches by using different fruits instead of blueberries: For Apple Crunch use 4 apples, peeled, cored, and sliced; for Strawberry Crunch use 2 cups strawberries, cut in half; for Peach Crunch use 2 cups sliced peaches. Can you think of other fruit crunches to make?

Doc's Caramel Apples

An apple a day keeps the doctor away—except if the doctor likes apples as much as Doc likes these caramel apples!

What you need:

½ cup chopped walnuts or peanuts

5 small apples

5 wooden ice-cream sticks

1 package (14 ounces) chewy vanilla caramels

1 tablespoon water

What you do with it:

1. Line a cookie sheet with waxed paper. Empty the nuts onto it and divide them into 5 equal heaps. Make sure to leave lots of space between the heaps.

2. Wash and dry the apples. Twist off the stems (if they still have them). Push a wooden ice-cream stick about halfway into each apple in the same place the stem was.

3. Unwrap the caramels and put them and the water in the top of a double boiler. Fill the bottom of the double boiler with about 2 inches of water. Put the double boiler together and place it over medium heat.

4. Heat the caramels until they're melted and smooth, stirring every once in a while. Remove the double boiler from the heat.

5. Holding an apple by the stick, dip it into the caramel to coat it. Use a spatula or table knife to help cover the whole apple. Put the apple stick-side up on a heap of nuts, turning it so all the nuts stick to it. Coat the other apples the same way. (If the caramel gets too stiff, put the double boiler back on the heat for a few minutes.)

6. Refrigerate the apples until the caramel is firm, about ½ hour.

Serves 5.

To microwave:
Follow steps 1 and 2 above. Instead of steps 3 and 4, place unwrapped caramels in a 2-quart bowl. Add 2 tablespoons water and microwave on HIGH 3 to 4 minutes, just until caramels start to melt. Stir with a wooden spoon until the mixture is smooth. Continue as directed in steps 5 and 6.

Minnie Mouse's Tropical Treat

What you need:

4 canned pineapple rings

4 scoops orange, lemon, or lime sherbet

2 tablespoons shredded coconut

4 maraschino cherries or 4 whole strawberries

What you do with it:

1. Put 1 pineapple ring in each of 4 dessert dishes.

2. Place 1 scoop of sherbet on top of each pineapple ring.

3. Sprinkle the coconut over the sherbet.

4. Place 1 cherry or strawberry on top of each portion.

Serves 4.

Chip and Dale's Nutty Fruit Cup

What you need:

1 banana
1 or 2 scoops orange sherbet
1 tablespoon crushed peanuts
2 tablespoons orange juice

What you do with it:

1. Peel the banana and cut it into thin slices. Arrange them around the edge of a dessert dish.

2. Put the sherbet in the center of the dish.

3. Sprinkle the peanuts on top and drizzle with the orange juice.

Serves 1.

Sleeping Beauty's Spinning Wheels

Sleeping Beauty has dreamed up a truly scrumptious dessert!

What you need:

2 plain or chocolate-covered doughnuts

2 scoops ice cream (use your favorite flavor)

2 teaspoons chocolate sprinkles

What you do with it:

1. Place 1 doughnut in each of 2 dessert dishes.

2. Put 1 scoop of ice cream on top of each doughnut.

3. Sprinkle each scoop of ice cream with 1 teaspoon sprinkles.

Serves 2.

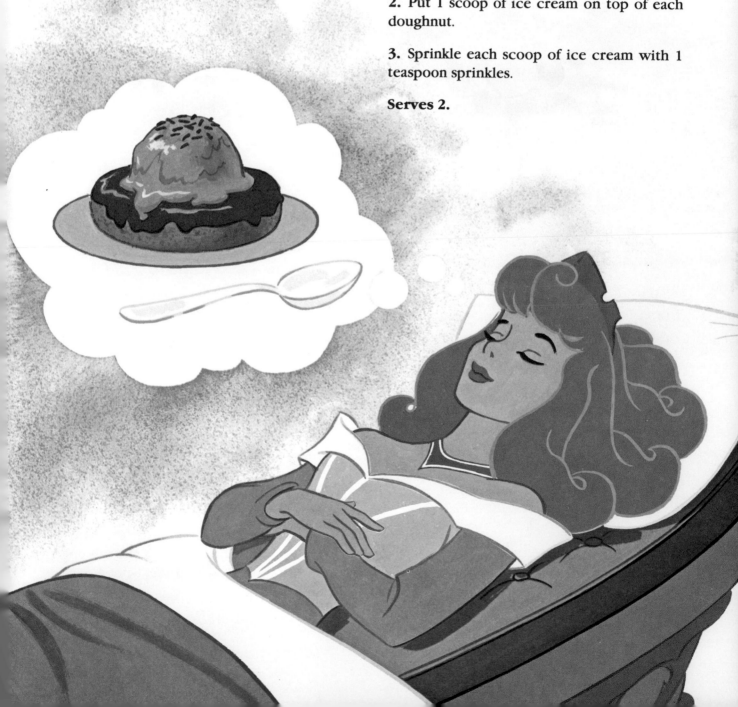

Tweedle Dum and Tweedle Dee's Banana Split

What you need:

2 bananas

4 scoops ice cream (use your favorite kind—and 2 flavors are even better)

4 tablespoons chocolate syrup

½ cup whipped cream or whipped topping

2 tablespoons chopped nuts

This recipe is a great place to use your imagination, since the only things you have to put in a banana split are bananas and ice cream. So if you can think of something else you'd rather use here, go right ahead. Maybe a different flavor syrup? Or some sprinkles? Or cut-up fruit? Or, or, or...

What you do with it:

1. Peel the bananas and slice them in half the long way. Put 2 halves on each of 2 plates.

2. Put 2 scoops ice cream down the center of each plate.

3. Spoon 2 tablespoons chocolate syrup over each portion.

4. Top each portion with half the whipped cream and sprinkle with 1 tablespoon nuts.

Serves 2.

Morty and Ferdie's Snowballs

These are much better for eating than for throwing.

What you need:

½ cup shredded coconut

2 teaspoons chocolate sprinkles

1 pint ice cream (any flavor you like)

Snowballs are terrific all by themselves, but you can also serve them on top of slices of cake, wedges of pie, or dishes of pudding or gelatin dessert.

What you do with it:

1. Put the coconut and spinkles in a square baking pan, 8x8x2 inches. Mix them together.

2. With an ice-cream scoop, make 4 balls of ice cream (try to make them as round as possible). Place the balls in the baking pan.

3. Using 2 spoons, roll the balls around until each one is coated with the coconut mixture.

4. Lift each ball out of the pan with the spoons and into a dessert dish. Put the dishes in the freezer for 10 minutes so that the ice cream can get good and hard again.

Serves 4.

AGES

Nana's Hot Cocoa

Nana knows that this is just the thing to quiet down her charges in the Darling nursery so that they'll be ready for bed after a hard evening of let's pretend.

What you need:

1 heaping teaspoon unsweetened cocoa powder

2 heaping teaspoons sugar

1 cup milk

What you do with it:

1. Put the cocoa and sugar into a cup. Gradually stir in 2 teaspoonfuls of the milk. Stir to make a paste.

2. Pour the rest of the milk into a small saucepan. Heat it over low heat just until a few tiny bubbles form around the edge of the saucepan.

3. Pour the milk into the cup and stir very well.

Serves 1.

Some people like a marshmallow or two in their cocoa, melting into foamy delight. Others like a spoonful of whipped cream or whipped topping—it's lovely to sip the steaming cocoa through the icy-cold cream.

Maid Marian's Mulled Cider

This hot and spicy cider keeps everybody warm on cold nights in Sherwood Forest.

What you need:

1 quart apple cider or juice

½ cup brown sugar

½ teaspoon whole cloves

1 small cinnamon stick

⅛ teaspoon nutmeg

Juice of ½ lemon

5 or 6 small orange slices

What you do with it:

1. Pour the apple cider into a large heatproof glass, enamel, or stainless steel saucepan. Add the rest of the ingredients except the orange slices.

2. Heat over low heat for 20 to 30 minutes or until the cider starts to simmer. Remove from the heat and take out the cinnamon stick and cloves with a spoon.

3. Ladle into mugs or heatproof glasses to serve. Put an orange slice on top of each serving.

Serves 5 or 6.

Dumbo's Double-Thick Chocolate Malted

Dumbo, being an elephant, doesn't need a straw to drink this. Kids aren't that lucky.

What you need:

½ cup milk

2 scoops chocolate ice milk or ice cream

3 tablespoons chocolate-flavor malted milk

What you do with it:

1. Pour the milk into a small mixing bowl. Add 1 scoop ice cream. Beat with an eggbeater until the ice cream is mixed in.

2. Add the rest of the ice cream and the malted milk. Beat again until the mixture is foamy. Pour into a glass to serve.

Serves 1.

Goofy's Banana Milk Shake

What you need:

1 banana

1½ cups milk

¼ teaspoon vanilla extract

What you do with it:

1. Peel the banana and break it into chunks with your fingers. Put the chunks in a medium bowl and mash them with a fork until there are no lumps left.

2. Pour in the milk and vanilla. Beat with an eggbeater until the shake is smooth and foamy. Pour into 2 glasses to serve.

Serves 2.

Shere Khan's Orange Float

What you do:

1. For each person that you want to serve, place 1 scoop vanilla ice cream in a tall glass.

2. Pour in enough orange juice to fill the glass. Stir the float a couple of times with a spoon.

You can make a float with any flavor fruit juice. And what about using sherbet instead of the ice cream? Just for starters, try pineapple juice with chocolate sherbet—then go on from there yourself.

Baloo's Root Beer Float

What you do:

1. For each person that you want to serve, place 1 scoop vanilla ice cream in a tall glass.

2. Pour in enough root beer to fill the glass. Stir until the ice cream is half melted.

Donald Duck's Ice-Cream Soda

Donald's recipe is better than his aim—see if *you* can get the ice cream in the glass.

What you need:

4 tablespoons chocolate syrup

Seltzer water

2 scoops ice cream (any flavor you like)

What you do with it:

1. Put 2 tablespoons chocolate syrup in each of 2 tall glasses.

2. Fill each glass about one quarter full with seltzer water. Mix well with a spoon.

3. Add 1 scoop ice cream to each glass, then fill with seltzer water.

Serves 2.

The White Rabbit's Gingerapple Fizz

This is so quick to fix that even the White Rabbit has time enough to stop rushing and make one.

What you need:

1 cup apple juice

2 scoops vanilla ice cream

1 can (12 ounces) ginger ale

What you do with it:

1. Pour ½ cup apple juice into each of 2 tall glasses.

2. Add 1 scoop ice cream to each glass.

3. Fill the glasses with the ginger ale. Stir.

Serves 2.

Index

Main Dishes

Applesauce-Topped Ham, Donald Duck's, 58
Macaroni and Cheese, Mickey Mouse's Microwave, 60
Magic Fried Chicken, Merlin's, 59
Meat Loaf, Archimedes', 57
Pasta, Peter Pan's, 54
Spaghetti and Chickenballs, Lady and the Tramp's, 56
Spaghetti Sauce, Tinker Bell's, 55
Tuna-Noodle Casserole, Thumper's, 61

Pancakes, French Toast, and Waffles

French Toast, Winnie the Pooh's, 47
    Cheese, Tigger's, 47
    Jam, Eeyore's, 47
    Peanut Butter, Owl's, 47
    Sandwich, Open-Face, Christopher Robin's, 47
Oatmeal Pancakes, Wonderland, 44-45
    Applesauce, the Dormouse's, 45
    Cheese, the Cheshire Cat's, 45
    Chocolate, the White Rabbit's, 45
    Hot Dog, the March Hare's, 45
    Jelly Roll, the Queen of Hearts', 45
    Peanut Butter, Tweedle Dum and Tweedle Dee's, 45
Waffles, 46

Salads

Fruit Salad, King Louie's, 71
Garden Salad, Bambi's, 69
Tuna Fish Salad, O'Malley's, 70

Sandwiches

Cheeseburgers, Scrooge McDuck's, 34
Grilled Cheese Sandwich, Cinderella's, 36
Hamburgers, Donald Duck's, 34
Hot Dogs, Pluto's Chicken, 35
Meat Sandwich, Robin Hood's, 39
Peanut Butter Sandwich Deluxe, Dumbo's, 38
Pizza Muffins, Piglet's, 37
Triple-Decker Sandwich, Chip and Dale's, 39

Soups

Beanie-Weenie Soup, Mickey Mouse's, 41
Pea Soup with Cheese Crackers, Pinocchio's, 40
Vegetable Soup, Baloo's Microwave, 40
Yankee Noodle Dandy, Jiminy Cricket's, 41

Vegetables

Baked Potatoes, Daisy Duck's, 68
Carrots, Brer Rabbit's, 64
Corn on the Cob, the Caterpillar's, 64
Green Beans, Grumpy's, 65
Mashed Potatoes, Captain Hook's, 66